RETURN
FLIGHT

RETURN FLIGHT

Poems

JENNIFER HUANG

MILKWEED EDITIONS

Published 2022 by Milkweed Editions
Printed in the United States of America
Cover design by Mary Austin Speaker
Cover art by María Medem
22 23 24 25 26   6 5 4 3 2
First Edition

Library of Congress Cataloging-in-Publication Data

Names: Huang, Jennifer, author.
Title: Return flight : poems / Jennifer Huang.
Description: First edition. | Minneapolis, Minnesota : Milkweed Editions,
    2022. | Summary: "Selected by Jos Charles as the winner of the 2021
    Ballard Spahr Prize for Poetry, Return Flight is a lush reckoning: with
    inheritance, with body, with trauma, with desire-and with the many
    tendons in between"-- Provided by publisher.
Identifiers: LCCN 2021037273 (print) | LCCN 2021037274 (ebook) |
    ISBN 9781571315281 (trade paperback) | ISBN 9781571317179
    (ebook)
Subjects: LCGFT: Poetry.
Classification: LCC PS3608.U2248 R48 2022 (print) | LCC PS3608.
    U2248 (ebook) | DDC 811/.6--dc23
LC record available at https://lccn.loc.gov/2021037273
LC ebook record available at https://lccn.loc.gov/2021037274

Milkweed Editions is committed to ecological stewardship. We strive to align our book production practices with this principle, and to reduce the impact of our operations in the environment. We are a member of the Green Press Initiative, a nonprofit coalition of publishers, manufacturers, and authors working to protect the world's endangered forests and conserve natural resources. *Return Flight* was printed on acid-free 100% postconsumer-waste paper by McNaughton & Gunn.

For family.

And that which is unsaid.

Contents

Return Flight

Neighborhood Walk

A crop of deer appears. They kiss
the cheek of my periphery.
I open to let them pass. From the edge
I hear: ni shi huan ma? kuai le ma?
A father and daughter ride a bike,
and on the handlebars, their hands,
their hands! touch like a long goodbye.

Departure

The things I don't know have stayed

In this home. I look out to a nothing sky.
I am learning to fly before I speak.

Learned to fly before I could speak.
Before I could speak, I was left behind.

What I couldn't express, was left behind.
I leave behind the things that don't belong

To me. The red life vest floating out to sea.

Customs

"What language conceals is said through my body."
—ROLAND BARTHES

I touched everything, but the more I touched, I learned,
　　the more I broke. Like the time with the stairwell bannister,
　　　　that spot already on its way. I just helped it to its fate.
　　　　　　My father saw and warned he'd break my arm, leaving
　　　　me to wonder if my arm was mine or his.
There's more but if I translated all he said, it would sound
sweeter. My brother, the one to come and soothe. My brother,
　　years later also the one to hit me while I was watching TV—
　　　　a smack interrupting and a sudden welt on my back.
　　　　　　My breath was gone. Funny, how I can forgive my brother,
　　　　not my father for teaching him. And no, I can't praise my father
for never hitting me—his threats, a metronome keeping my life
in rhythm. If I try hard enough, I can forget but
　　a part of me wishes to keep my hand on these memories,
　　　　to feel them to their ends. Earlier today, I touched
　　　　　　a hot pan and dropped my dinner, then flinched
　　　　as I waited for the voice. Once, I let a lover
place his hands around my throat. I don't want
to like it. My body, powerless with another;
　　forgiveness before I can even shape the words.

Disaster

after Typhoon Morakot

On the drive to Alishan, zipping up
and up in the storm, father feared
the landslides that could bury us.
Even after ten years, Xiaolin Village
was ruin. I collapsed when I saw

the home after the divorce. Running
into memories exhausted my father.
What was left of my room was the blue bed
I hated. In the living room, statues carved
from cypresses I will one day inherit.

Fantasy Self-Erasure

It's ok

                             I forget

I forget

                      I miss

                Sorry

                    what is wrong

       with   desire

                      I step through
      your front door, take off my shoes
    and coat, and find you

between then and now

          here   hands
      hands

  me
       still   me

That dawn at the beach

I saw a sika turn into a shark.
He plodded to the edge of the earth.
When the wind shifted, he noticed
me in the dark and dove
into the water, his legs
soaring to the heavens
and his tail becoming an arced fin.
He caught waves like I used to
catch my father in prayer
giving his soft away. I want
to be seen like that.
Now, the sting of incense
is a ceremony of beasts
who shift to fit the morning.

Notes on Orange

In case you're wondering, the fruit came first,
the color name second. They called it red-yellow
for some time, and for some time it was just that.
Red brought nearer to humanity by yellow, as
Kandinsky described it. I am just that: a human
who wants to be closer to god. What is the true
opposite of human? Maybe orange. A piece of
sun, its properties have been known to help us
recall the feeling of cool-blue grass under toes, the
chime of a baby robin, the holy scent of ripe mud.
What is it that makes us want to get close? To the
gods, to summer, to sweetness, before we retreat
again, before we

desire again. It comes hungry in the night when I
wake to sweet citrus stuck in my fingernails and
remember the way I eat oranges as if I had known
you. Cutting eight sections. Cutting each fibrous top.
Sticking my fingers into flesh to extract the seeds.
This is how you did it, too—grandfather, a figment
of my imagination. An angry god brought closer
to me by my mother. She named him father, dear,
clown, monster, storm, sunfish, flesh, love—love!
If forgiveness is an absence, I make a tent with my
fingers and bow to his sweet-sour spritzing over me
like a bloom, I bloom.

Tanka

My mother dances
above the ripples. A dark
carp kisses her feet.
Grandfather takes my hand; leads
me into the Potomac.

Our clothes dry on the
line; the ghosts of our bodies
bend with high noon's light.
We are dragonflies waiting
for the falling rain to fall.

haiku

purple half-moon scar
running down the stairs to see
mess on every branch

our mouth can't move us
away from the scene a bowl
blossoming open

our father beating
the dirt out of the carpet
and wringing the laugh

from the house grew his
silences louder until
his hand spoke our name

and shook the new pears
off their branches he controls
the weather he makes

the breeze the rain feels
like blessing from gods the sun
a beautiful flare

until it burns our
skin nine shades of scarlet: a
cardinal in flight

Procedure

I wear the gown wrong so I can't be touched.
But the doctor, delicate in her asking, asks me
To open. I am not accustomed to this gentle;
I crush it. It is summer here. These walls
Fluorescent white so light I can feel me burn.
The doctor and a body. The vinegar
She puts inside me. I glue a mouth
To this heart. She wants to cut me apart.
No, she wants to cut a part from me,
Hold cotton until I clot. On the wall:
Laughing child splashed by water. *I am*
Aware of my heart. I count my blessings:
Three missed calls, two mirrors, one bouquet.
I am numb. Then I touch some place low.

228

When I first learned about 228 (recounting
this I am ashamed) I thought—
finally, an explanation; a name.

A son lifts up the bloodied undershirt with holes
that had been taken off his father post-
execution. He looks into the camera

and presses his mouth into a half smile. Maybe
one day the smell of lilies won't remind him of death.
The room welcomes a breeze. It rises.

Don't be sad. I never wanted my photo to be taken;
to kill the child within. In defiance
rose a desire to be nothing.

Departure

My father used to pick baby bok choy sprouts and place them in my bowl. I don't remember exactly when he stopped, but I miss those dinners when grown-ups would fight to pay—sometimes pretending to go to the bathroom but really grabbing the check. We would choke down our food to get seconds though there was always plenty. Slurping and clanking took place of conversation until the table was left a wreck. My father and I would share what we called the *best parts* of the fish—the cheeks and neck—and suck the meat from the bones. He would cut a spoonful, place sweet-brothed ginger and scallions atop, and tell me, *Chew slowly and feel what you are eating.* Once, I realized a bone was stuck in my throat. The skeleton clawed my speech—*why didn't I listen?* My brother fed me vinegar-doused rice. I took it, swallowed every bite and bit through acid nausea, and gradually, from my throat it dissolved further, within, without evidence.

From the Taiwan Cypress in Alishan

it's true	half of us have disappeared
they say	our fragrance is that of god
we can't help	we wail for the lost
family	axed down for profit
	their knives scratch our surface
sometimes they walk	beneath our shadows
after dusk searching	for something we
our spirits	dissipate and become

Individualism

At Lowe's, a store clerk helps me
cut a sheet of plexiglass, his hands
pulling the blade as he tells me
he quit school when he realized
creative writing wouldn't earn him
money. I laugh at the irony
as I admit my field of study.

On the way out, glass in hand,
the smell of hotdogs makes me recall
those Lowe's trips dad and I would take,
how I'd walk with him through the aisles
feeling small. He would lecture me
about earnings, property, and stocks;
the importance of making a living

and saving. Creativity was a *luxury*
he never had. Afterwards, he would hand me
a treat: a soft pretzel and hotdog.
A hard day's work always ended
with nourishment. I never felt empty
in that way. His hands were gentle
when I called him *babi* instead of *baba*.

When I start my car, I remember
how he used to pinch my cheeks
until I grew out of it, until I shied away,
learning touch could also mean *purple,*
blue, baby—then notice how the radio
continues playing the song I had
heard when I first stepped out.

Disorder

Mo-sin-a could never confuse me
the way they did my aunt.
I was good compared to her. Good

in my father's eyes meant I was good
in God's. I could always find
my way back from the woods,

but never from the devils in my head.
They wiggle their tongue in my ear
and spit my name in the dirt.

There, a buttercup blooms until
plucked by a hand pushing the yellow
to my chin. My body obeys, glows.

A Visit from Brother Ghost on the Harvest Moon

Brother, a window I lie below tonight.
Mother moon motioning minds away at night.

What I know of him is what I've been told
on highways in the slow middle of the night

from a mouth too tired. The truth rolls out
a story sitting tight on the throat. The knife-

edge, moonlight slicing through him,
across me. I fear I'll forget this. Tonight

I recite every detail to make a memory. How
can I love someone I've never known? At night,

what I know is what I imagine: brother, alive.
Wave and gravity pulling me to him. My knight.

Once, he called *Chia Chia* and I found my way.
Now, my hands holding his pane all night.

for Tai Shen, Goddess and Spirit Protector of the Unborn Child

I fear the baby
before it even arrives
can't move or fix or
clean anything I can
feel it watching
or is it that I fear
for the baby a new
moon thought
I must send away
only think
of the sun
the light I think
I can feel the baby
its spirit dances
under the bed
my husband is sound
a breathing lullaby
turned away from me
I can't fall asleep
I can feel the baby
in our closet I woke up
and couldn't find
any red I wish
this baby to be
gone too late baby
already hates me mother
stays in the room next door
she only feeds the rich

heavens to me
all I want is duck
and watermelon iced
water cold to soothe
my sweat my tired I am
only allowed to think
pleasant thoughts
see pleasant things
though not the needle
thread not the hammer
nail baby in the laundry
room baby is not
the knives not the baby
in the oven the moving
sky baby waits by
the door such a beauty
this dark-damp cave
there is no door
there such a beauty

poem for giving birth

my mother, my moon, myth
by moonlight, mates mirror to mirror.

her mirror: a heart, a humming chest, a heart
humming a heart, a child. my mirror: my empty

she empties into. my mine, my mind, morning. who is
the mirror's mother? moaning i mourn a dream: my mother

in another mother's body and me, my own mother. i build a moat,
oar to meet a mountain i mine. i myth a mess of myself. my mother

mouths a hymn masked, unmasked by a monsoon casting shadow
to shore. black hole in this smothered weather. messy, this mist,

this moisture, my spore slicking thin between firs, this sky.
mother, mud and muck, my guide! thinly veiled ghost

i try to muster and master. every night, her mirror
somewhere reflecting fire i turn to aster.

Among a sea of clouds

the palm trees walk. Creating landslides and slowing us down, the
storms last a week. Everywhere, gray ghosts we do not fear.

Prayers howl like the sea devouring mountaintops. We wait to eat. On this
weather we feed, Ah-gong always last. He blesses

the table with bamboo and pork tongue and ginger sprouts and insists
dou chi wan, nothing to be left for him.

Thick fog of incense rolls over us as we bow down to the rice, to Mazu,
Tudigong, wafting till all we see is what we hold,

a bowl. A hand rumbles, thunder bringing a pot of pu-er—Ah-gong,
whose heaven-black eyes ring the turquoise of Sun

Moon Lake. Blues turn green to a hazy splatter of chaos. Even when it
pours, his smile curves a slow wave, shimmers till I can't feel my hunger.

Turbulence

Many visitors lately. I wake
to an ache in my sternum.

Washing dishes, I cry
without cause. What pain is

the desire for pain?

Ode to Menstruation

Envelope, luck and offering

placed beneath the pillow; forget

then find again in the coming

of the night. Dream a dim voice,

a prophecy of profit slick

between fingers. Awake to palms,

open wounds painting

money on sheets; rosy

cheeks spilled from

lips. Balsamic moon

on white, drip.

The Creek

Here, reckless, unplanned life—a secret
hiding place where you let me stick my toes in.

You tell me how you and mother picked our home
because of this creek, then choose a branch to give

to me—my hiking staff for years to come. You
take one for yourself. From then on, we brush

aside weeds, making sure to put them back
in place. Sheltered by our canopy, we walk until

I don't want to be seen with you anymore.

Pleasure Practice

I am aligning myself with pleasure. This means daily I pray
for theirs—my neighbors who fuck loud.
They fight the same. I learn the sound
is better than the silence after. Stars as I try to see
straight when I rise from knees

too swiftly. Hands like rainfall.
This is not what I imagined. A man and I
once kissed in his car
until we didn't. *Enough*, he said,

pulling away. Was my greed
or desire too big to hold?
Truth is I didn't want a man. Really,

I want to feel all of me
realize what is, what is;

my body, in existence; *enough*.

Layover

Taiwan is written *all over*
your face, the 7-Eleven clerk says
at check-out. His name, that of a gem: Topaz, who's been
to Kaohsiung, Guangdong, Fujian, Shanghai, Beijing—
I have never been. *Your places,*
he says and I bristle at the mixing,
though delighted by my face: a map
I apparently can't hide. The shame,
then, at my delight:
I just want to be close.

Back in a house, this map devours
softness: a spoonful
of coffee-flavored san-yi
melting on the tongue
and into me. Then, a memory:

> tsua-bing and ai-yu
> to cool the climate—
> everywhere, bodies
> sweating into one.

Do I do, to Taiwan,
as the man does to me.

In a dressing room, little girl learns how to cinch a belly with her hands

and say: I'm lucky, I look good in anything. Mother's

love is a sacrifice. Little girl dresses,

then undresses, eyes closed;

avoids this body,

grieved.

Little girl, you
are hands clasped in
prayer; broken
straw; tall
seagrass;
a head above
the Pacific; melting
ice cube; curious
fool; a girl;
any girl browsing
a store looking
for ancestors;
too many
questions;
a tongue; captive;
captivated.

Taiwan is a feather;
first and third
quarter moon;
an angled leaf;
peace lily;
papaya;
mango pit,
chewed and slick;
pinky nail; profile
of Ah-jie's nose
before he turns
to me; cracked
seashell; lobster
claw; getting lost
in green brush
then seeing
the sea.

                           the mountains have different faces. The
magic   the motorbikes flee past
                    I
                  tangled in   half-say

              stuck

                                                      I can't
speak   without
                        red pen

                                                      I
forgot my   abandoned   sentence
               load of accuracy

                                        The death   makes
me cry   every red thing: hong kuai
                  the air of their branches

I closed my eyes to become a different face.

The distance between me and I grew

So you could love me as you've

Always imagined. I thought

That's what you wanted.

Then, distance be-

Came infinite.

I opened.

Formosa
they name
when they mark

your mountains
your green green
blues flooding red

earth surrounded
by seas *beautiful*
island they called

you *free China*
in the paper
you conquered

now *ungrateful*
child what name do
you crown yourself

I am mountain, storm, water-dust.
Those who come rarely know

when to leave. Go ahead—

call me naïve, then see:
these winds, turning, carry justice.

stray cat under stove

steaming sausages on a wok

smoke above the koi pond

green moss stuck on heel

father's tongue stamping

I am American to taxi driver

stepping over to enter

the red temple

baibai baibai

naked in the bathhouse

some ah-ma cooing

You look like my granddaughter

thank her with tears

the moldy window

you turn to and notice

outside two papayas touch

TAIPEI, MAY 2019

Departure

We pick wet flowers and mix them into the tire-indents
where our parents' cars should be. This is flower stew.
We play pretend: I am the robin and she is the blue jay.
We play reality: I am the tire and she is the car.
Her parents no longer sleep together and neither do mine.
At dusk, we part. I run up the stairs. My mind is always faster
than my body. Mother sees the scrapes on my knees
and tries to beat me with a wire hanger. It never reaches
flesh. Still, I can never walk past a sharp corner
without bruising myself. I climb the monkey bars
at midnight. *Sorry doesn't mean a thing, never laugh
too hard, always think ahead*—this is the bedtime story
my father reads to me. I recite it by memory
as I squeeze my frame through the bars, climb on top
of the rungs, then stand. I laugh too hard, then jump down.

After the Storm

Born again some moment between my waking breath and my body caving into
    its own shutters. 7:11 a.m. Devil's ivy creeps up the thighs of a body

I know. There was a time when I was afraid to go to sleep for fear of never
    waking up. Then, Ah-ma told me I could fly.

And I know I am evergreen. I am leaving me. Yes,

again, I lost my body and found it under the mattress.

The yoga instructor says to *feel the ground hold you up.* I fear the world most

in these moments. I make like a kite, let the wind hold me up. The sun cracks
    my skin till I tatter. There was a time when all I could think of was
    getting back to sleep. In a dream,

I am not in a dream. Hands tingling, Ah-ma reels me back, patches me up.

song of chou doufu

a smell before you see & taste—my foul like a hand reaching dimensions
beyond human comprehension. I waft a ballad so ancient, so perfect

you'll pray to forget me, exceed me, belittle me. alas, my stench soaks you
a waterfall of rotting garbage you can't rinse out. I am a parade of wet socks,

cheese, & moldy feet. relish my complexities: can you taste what bathed me?
mother brine flaunted this way of being *too much*; they say I am *too much*,

their protests only making my reek louder, happier—joyful stench!
when they discovered me, it was like newton & gravity. they fell

hard & fast. I kill *soft*, delicious. you could only be so lucky,
so lucky to taste this wicked love. eat me! o, eat me & be blessed.

Self-Pleasure

I think of him when I touch myself;
Imagine that I am riding a god,

Because he was not just any man.
He was the first to talk to me about god

So bright I tasted the divine when we kissed.
It's tiring, turning men into gods.

I'm tired of seeing the world
As a constant reflection. I forgot

That the icicles don't cry because of
The slickness between my thighs. *Oh, god.*

How to Love a Rock

Notice the maroon cirrus clouds against
the gray of her landscape, then each white spot—
stars that propel you into space. Tell her
what you see, how you love the way

she smells like grass and salt. Ask about her
properties, history, how she was picked
from the glacial waters of Lake Crescent
and brought across the land to be placed

in your palms. Ask to feel her smooth. Caress
till your thumb can find a home in her brook.
Be with her and share your day, how you jumped
into a river, came out ice. How you

worry now, let it go. Give her space to
say not words; then, when she's ready, many.

On Days I Stay with My Father

We walk the dog in circles,
let him play and roam
the tennis courts, though

the sign says *no dogs allowed*.
I can never remember your face
because I was often looking

at the ground when you yelled
so bright. But today, at the courts,
I carry my gaze to see you:

soft wrinkles and eyes like flame
asking for forgiveness. Or
perhaps, I, wanting. We laugh

at the dog prancing, and I want
to let our laughter mean just that—
a laugh. The past is faraway

though sometimes it stalks close.
The dog rolls over, lets the sun
touch his belly—then us.

Relief

a clock spins on my chest

      treasure I find underneath my fingers

nails that once hung a heart

      my heart sent to me by a goddess

goddess is the wind that blows my skirt

      the pleats limp *okay*

okay, this is yours to hold

      too, held once, as a baby

I yell and mimic a mustang

      the horses gallop on the landscape

of my thighs, I draw

      the blinds close to hear

what is private

Nonconcordant

When you ask to watch hentai
together, your fingers
already typing, I can't stop myself
from not-speaking and then from not-
watching the screen held by a hand
that, just an hour ago, held mine
across a table before our food arrived,
and that now sweats as we watch
what I did not want
and hear what I think
is pleasure ringing, and I wonder
what exactly led us to this moment,
when only three hours ago, I told
you a secret and you cradled
me in silence after my insides swelled
from a biopsy, until
some sound brings me back to me
watching us watching it and feeling
a wave I don't or can't understand—
and then my voice, asking for it
to end, surprising even me.

Tongue-Tied

In Ah-gong's apartment, lights off and lying
on our tatami, father tells me a story his mother told him:
There was one day when my uncle—you've never met him—
somehow fell into the water. When our family found him
lakeside and wet, he recalled how he saw white
and gray wisps wrap around him underwater.
Spirits had tried to drown him until the shadow of
an old man with a long beard reached in to pull him up.
He believed Tudigong saved him. We don't question
the times our family has been saved. Back then,
silence meant fortune and while my father was hit for speaking
Taiwanese, my mother still feels shame for not knowing it. *Wai-sheng ren*
taunts her. She, the one to teach me *Taiwan,*
Taiwanese, refuses to go to her parent-land. I hold both
under my tongue. When I tell father that I want to live
in Taiwan, he laughs: *Why?*
I bite. Forty years he's lived in America,
so when the taxi driver asks, *are you from here?*
he replies, *no, I am an American.*
That night, before we turned away to sleep, my father added:
Who knows if this story is real, but that uncle had no reason to lie.

Drift

I wanted this poem to be about dropping textbooks on my arm to get out of practicing violin. To be about grandfather hitting mom, and how decades later, I could still feel the sting. About ancestors changing their last name to *Guang*. But instead,

this poem wants to be about dad's beet face when he has exactly one drink; how, outside of a Paris café, glasses of wine in hand, brother and I glow like that one Van Gogh painting. It wants to be about mom wafting prayers as she stirs ribs and radishes and cauliflower in a pot for hours. The poem becomes the prayers,

and the prayers become my body. The body, I notice, plays a symphony, the stomach grumbling, and becomes the act of crusting salmon with miso and putting it in the convection oven I got

from a dear friend. The presence of beating hearts through objects passed down: Beanie Baby, moonstones, tarot deck, calendula oil, coffee grinder, cactus. It finally stretches to the South-facing window.

Zuihitsu for Yushan

I open my eyes to let him go.

At twenty, when drafting my first poem about Taiwan, I wrote:
*Where I am from / summer comes like a man / watching me, I am no
longer human*—Back then, the speaker was always me, the poet. I
wrote what I knew.

I live in a perpetual state of *I don't know* is what you once said to me.

Imagine what I don't know, I don't know.

just thin breeze black hair / short nails high grass dirt-/colored rain—
this discomfort was my peace. If I had known then what was
still to come.

One possible title for this poem: "Mountain Splitting."

I Google it and find a Chinese myth. (The algorithm works.) It
goes like this: a goddess falls in love with a mortal. Eventually they
marry and the goddess bears a half-god son. Then, from heaven,

the goddess's brother becomes furious and decides to imprison her inside a lotus-like mountain peak.

When the son grows up and learns this story, he travels to look for his mother. He meets a Daoist master, who trains him and gives him a magical ax. With it, he defeats his uncle in combat and splits open the mountain to free the goddess, his mother.

I don't know if they rejoice. This part has not yet been written.

I write this from a stranger's house, his cat sitting next to me. Twice a day, I fill up Bruno's bowl, and three times, I check his litterbox. I don't feel lost even though I must find the spatula, remote, coffee mug, towel. I admire the jade plant by the window. A wish to cradle a leaf green between my fore and thumb, feel its curves.

Q: Why the impulse to bring back an old poem?

A: I do not believe in the concluding lines, *is not where I am from. I am not from / not where I am from I am not.*

Q: Why the impulse to traverse old habits?

A: I believe in the refusal to explain.

I have done it again. I made a man my mountain and burrowed inside.

I write this from a coffee shop, holding Tina Chang's *Hybrida*. It is becoming evident that jades follow me. Their green touches me blue. What else touches? The lines at the end of "Fury":

> love and love and love and love and love
> and love and love and love and love and

my mind, a cat I try to call down.

This morning, I wore blood-scent and a face. I put distance between this man and me, love and me, I and me.

One origin of the verb *to know* means "to experience, live through" or "to have sexual intercourse with."

Is loving someone accepting the unknown?

I climb the mountain, this man. His rocks I get close to—I could kiss. I take my ax and almost split. I stop, instead, to hear the child of myself inside reciting: *Where I am from / everyone is family except for me.*

Unborrowed from rocks and salt and dirt and root, where I go from here, I don't know.

When I was on Alishan, I woke at 4 a.m. to take a train to then walk to the top; climbed it to see other mountains.

Across from me, the trees split your image, sliced again by the rising sun. Yushan, named for the way the snow makes you translucent like

a jade. My stone
around your neck.

I could almost
touch you. I did

by not.

Manifest

And when I reached the field,
it stopped me with a prophecy,
the bull with the human face.
I listened and thought

it was fate—I was to have
a life filled with cursed
love. I wandered on;
turned left and met a boy

who fucked me in the woods,
then another left, another boy
who showed me the Pac-Man
arcade in his parents' basement,

his arms muscular, his hands
maneuvering the mouth
around the maze, and I,
the ghost following.

A different path, a girl pleased with
her power over me, many moons,
while my shadow U-turned
for the boy who loved my silence,

silenced my love—silence,
I loved. Boy, who made me
sneak out the side. And girl,
who dealt drugs on our date.

I could see but couldn't stop. Living
as if I had no choice. I was
throwing myself until the path
pulled me back—to the bull.

Laughter. Then mine, bursting
from my lips. A cry as I caressed
a sun-wet afternoon. For only
I was left and then I left.

Notes

I have returned after a life of wandering; you lie uneasily
looking up. Yes, suppose this time
we use your perspective as the vantage point, this time
when I, a survivor, bend forward from the edge and look down . . .
—FROM "LOOKING DOWN" BY YANG MU,
TRANS. BY MICHELLE YEH & LAWRENCE R. SMITH

In Taiwanese: *Ah-ma* is paternal grandmother; *Ah-gong* is paternal grandfather; *Ah-jie* is a father's younger brother, or uncle. **In Mandarin:** *Baba* is father.

"Departure [The things I don't know]" is written after "Duplex" by Jericho Brown and "Pulling the Moon" by Marcelo Hernandez Castillo.

"That dawn at the beach" and **"Manifest"** are poems based on Taiwanese ghost and spirit stories I read in 妖怪台灣 by 何敬堯 (*Yaoguai Taiwan* by Ho Ching-yao). Thank you, Mom, for translating these stories for me.

"Notes on Orange" was inspired by *The Secret Lives of Color* by Kassia St. Clair. This poem is for Yang Cheng.

"Procedure" takes a line from "Tulips" by Sylvia Plath.

February 28, 1947 (or 228) was the beginning of Taiwan's White Terror, or a period of martial law that lasted until 1987. "Official records" state that during this time, over 140,000 Taiwanese people were imprisoned and between 3,000 and 4,000 executed by the Chinese Nationalist Party (Kuomintang) led by Chiang Kai-shek. Other sources say that the numbers were much higher, including up to 28,000 deaths.

In **"228,"** two of the stanzas imagine the moments before Pan Hsin-hsing had his picture taken for the *South China Morning Post* article "70 years after Taiwan's 'White Terror', relatives of victims still seeking justice." The article mentions that lilies decorated the room of his father Pan Mu-chih's funeral and how, for many years after, Hsin-hsing could not stand the smell because they reminded him of that day. Pan Mu-chih was a doctor and local politician. In his last translated note, he had written on a cigarette pack: "Don't be sad, I die for the residents of our city. I die with no regret."

As heard from a tour guide: when the Japanese ruled Taiwan, they made expeditions to Alishan to harvest the Taiwan cypress, also known as **hong kuai**. They revered this tree for the quality of its wood, as well as its unique scent. As the Japanese logged more and more, they began to hear cries coming from the forest at night, but they could never find the source. They believed the trees were grieving and haunting them. To this day, because of overharvesting, the Taiwan cypress is considered endangered.

Mo-sin-a are devilish creatures that roam mountains, forests, and countrysides and enjoy playing tricks on children and elderly folks. Most commonly, they cause folks to lose their sense of direction, leaving them to wander around in circles. I grew up hearing stories about them from my dad.

In Chinese folk religion, there is a belief that during pregnancy, the Goddess **Tai Shen** will come to the house to watch over the fetus; she will sometimes even disguise herself as objects in the home. Others believe that Tai Shen is the spirit of the fetus that lives in the house, outside of the womb, and moves from object to object throughout the day. Both beliefs urge the importance of avoiding anything that might offend the spirit while carrying a child, such as moving or renovating the home, carrying heavy objects, sewing, eating yin (or "cold") foods, hammering nails, or hitting objects. Offending Tai Shen can cause miscarriage or illness.

"Among a sea of clouds" was written for Ah-gong. The title is taken from the Mandarin phrase yunhai, which directly translates to "cloud-sea" or "sea of clouds". Yunhai refers to the phenomenon of clouds settling lower than the mountain peaks and covering the land in a blanket of foggy mist. Getting caught in yunhai is a sought-after experience in Taiwan. These conditions are part of what creates the unique climate for Taiwanese high mountain tea.

In Chinese folk religion, **Tudigong** is the Lord of the Soil and Earth. **Mazu** is the Goddess and Patroness of the Sea; she is the deified form of the Fujianese shaman Lin Mo. Worship of Mazu is popular in Taiwan and rituals include the yearly Baishatun Mazu Pilgrimage, in which the statue of Mazu is carried in procession to Daoist temples around Taiwan. The journey is approximately four hundred kilometers.

"Layover" contains an erasure of a poem I wrote in my Notes app during a trip my dad and I took to Taiwan in May 2019. The original text detailed the inadequacies, shame, and exhaustion of having to communicate with language barriers.

San-yi literally translates to "three-one," which is used as a shorthand to refer to Baskin-Robbins and the company's thirty-one flavors. **Tsua-bing** is a shaved ice dessert popular in Taiwan. **Ai-yu** is a jelly, made from awkeotsang creeping fig seeds. In Taiwan, it is popular to eat the jelly with lime and sweeteners to cool the body down. **Baibai** is the act of prayer.

Chou doufu, also known as stinky tofu, is a dish made from fermented tofu and known for its strong odor. To me, and many others, this odor is a lure—a signal of delicious love.

"On Days I Stay with My Father" is a revision of a poem written first from a personalized prompt in a workshop with Diane Seuss. Thank you, Diane, for challenging me to observe with keener eyes.

"Relief" was written for Silver Lake and Pinckney Recreation Area in Michigan.

I first learned of **arousal nonconcordance** in *Come As You Are* by Emily Nagoski. Thank you to Abigail Bereola and Jishava Patel for our community that made this knowing possible.

"Tongue-Tied" takes from stories of my family's experience during Taiwan's period of martial law. **Wai-sheng ren** roughly translates to "mainlander." It has been used as a slur to distinguish between Taiwan "natives" (Taiwan ren) and the wave of immigrants (and their children born locally thereafter) who arrived from China in the 1940s (Wai-sheng ren). Above, I put natives in quotations because this group includes other, earlier immigrant waves—not only the Indigenous people of Taiwan.

In **"Zuihitsu for Yushan,"** the etymology of *to know* was found on etymonline.com. **Yushan**, or Jade Mountain, is the highest mountain in Taiwan, at almost thirteen thousand feet above sea level. My dad tells me it is the most dangerous to climb.

Gratitude

Many thanks to the editors and staff of the following publications, in which these poems, sometimes in different versions, first appeared:

Blueshift Journal, "Departure [We pick wet flowers]" (as "After the Storm");

The Journal, "poem for giving birth";

The Margins, "Zuihitsu for Yushan";

Narrative Magazine, "Nonconcordant";

On Loan from the Cosmos, "Procedure" and "taking breaths";

POETRY, "From the Taiwan Cypress in Alishan" and "A Visit from Brother Ghost on the Harvest Moon";

The Rumpus, "Return" (as "Customs"), "haiku," and "Pleasure Practice";

Sine Theta, "Among a sea of clouds";

Stone Pacific Zine, "After the Storm" (as "Disembodiment");

tenderness lit, "In a dream" (as "After the Storm");

underblong, "song of chou doufu" (as "song of 臭豆腐 (stinky tofu)");

Us Two Tea Voices, "Drift";

wildness, "How to Love a Rock."

An earlier version of "Departure [My father used to]" (as "Haibun for that which is left over") appeared in the University of Michigan Hopwood Program.

~

In 2017, I wrote in my journal: "I am always seeking home, I am starting to realize that one home does not exist. I think my home lies in moments. In myself. By the sea. Looking at a mountain. A sunset. Under the sheets. Under the stars. It's everywhere, yet nowhere."

This collection is, in part, a search for home—and the realization that *home* is not a destination but a journey. These poems are a look into some of the external and internal landscapes I encountered along the way. The search has not ended; the focus has only changed and evolved, and I am grateful for that. Thank you, reader, for witnessing this leg of the journey.

An unimaginably big thank you to my constellation of friends, many of whom have also been my first, trusty readers. Thank you for your steadfast love and support; for virtual coffees before it became a pandemic thing; for long phone calls when time disappears; for pulling cards and wondering together; for the times we laugh so hard it makes our stomach hurt; for including me in your backpack; for being down to be silly; for dancing and crying with me; for the times we sit-beside and witness each other. I love you so much.

Thank you to the generosity and resources of the Helen Zell Writers' Program at the University of Michigan, as well as the community of writers who have made my time in Michigan so nourishing. To my cohort, Poets Infinity—Joumana Altallal, Bryan Byrdlong, Aozora Brockman, Ian Burnette, Kassy Lee, Isabel Neal, Monica Rico, Michael Weinstein, Mariya

Zilberman—thank you for your support and for seeing my work so deeply. I couldn't have asked for better readers and friends.

I am grateful to have learned under such brilliant and caring professors, teachers, workshop leaders, and mentors: Jane Bernstein, Gerald Costanzo, Carrie Hagan, M. Stephanie Murray, Suzie Silver, Lauren Shapiro, Simone Kearney, Emily Skillings, Sarah Ensor, Linda Gregerson, Tung-Hui Hu, A. Van Jordan, Aliyah Khan, Khaled Mattawa, Diane Seuss, and Alex Barron. Thank you for believing in my creativity and for offering me seeds of curiosity to plant and nourish.

Thank you to the communities that have held space for me over the years: Sundog Lit, Taiwanese American Next Generation, The Writer's Center, North American Taiwan Studies Association, and others.

To Brooklyn Poets and the community of writers I met at yawps, classes, and impromptu workshops: thank you for helping me find my way back to the page. Thank you to the Yaysayers: Adrian Moens, Tess Congo, Corinna Munn, Kiran Bath, and Julia Knobloch. And thank you, Jason Koo, for your energy, generosity, and support.

To spiritual teachers and bodywork practitioners, who have held space for me so that I could come back to my body again and again: thank you for your presence and for the work that you do—the seen and unseeable.

Thank you to the therapists I have had over the years for supporting me in my healing journey.

To all my ex-lovers, and in the words of Ariana Grande: *thank u, next.*

To the incredible womxn I've had the chance to work with—you have each shown me ways to navigate the writing, publishing, and creative business worlds with ferocity, humor, bravery, and tenacity. Thank you.

Thank you, Jos Charles, for seeing something in these poems. Thank you to the Ballard Spahr Foundation for this opportunity. And thank you to the team at Milkweed: Daniel Slager, Bailey Hutchinson, Claire Laine, Broc Rossell, Yanna Demkiewicz, Milan Wilson-Robinson, Shannon Blackmer, Mary Austin Speaker, Meilina Dalit, and Tijqua Daiker. You all have been such a dream come true to work with.

I couldn't have done any of this without my family. Your love is where I often find my strength, support, and inspiration. Thank you to my extended family of cousins, aunts, uncles, and beyond. Thank you to Puo-Puo and Gong-Gong for always nurturing my creativity. Thank you, Mom, for your love and for being a safe place to be who I am. Thank you, Dad, for always being there and for giving me the tools to be grounded. To my brother Jonathan: thank you for being my first role model for reading and learning and for always being courageously you. Thank you to the elders and ancestors for all that you have lived.

To all the places I have been over the years—thank you for welcoming me and for gently letting me know when to say goodbye.

To Spirit, earth, sky, and universe: thank you for holding me when I feel alone, for all that you ask of me, for all that you give.

To my past selves—a part of you always believed in this book. Thank you for being exactly who you are—and for continuing, even when it was scary. I love you.

Ian Burnette

JENNIFER HUANG was born in Maryland to Taiwanese immigrants and has since called many places their home. Their poems have appeared in *POETRY*, *The Rumpus*, and *Narrative Magazine*, among other places; they have received recognition from the Academy of American Poets, Brooklyn Poets, North American Taiwan Studies Association, and more. In 2020, Huang earned their MFA in Poetry at the University of Michigan Helen Zell Writers' Program. A former resident of Michigan, they currently divide their time between Michigan, Maryland, and elsewhere.

The tenth award of
THE BALLARD SPAHR PRIZE FOR POETRY
is presented to
Jennifer Huang
by
MILKWEED EDITIONS
and
THE BALLARD SPAHR FOUNDATION

First established in 2011 as the Lindquist & Vennum Prize for Poetry, the annual Ballard Spahr Prize for Poetry awards $10,000 and publication by Milkweed Editions to a poet residing in Minnesota, Iowa, Michigan, North Dakota, South Dakota, or Wisconsin. Finalists are selected from among all entrants by the editors of Milkweed Editions. The winning collection is selected annually by an independent judge. The 2021 Ballard Spahr Prize for Poetry was judged by Jos Charles.

Milkweed Editions is one of the nation's leading independent publishers, with a mission to identify, nurture, and publish transformative literature, and build an engaged community around it. The Ballard Spahr Foundation was established by the national law rm of Ballard Sphar, LLC, and is a donor-advised fund of The Minneapolis Foundation.

Milkweed Editions, an independent nonprofit publisher, gratefully acknowledges sustaining support from our Board of Directors; the Alan B. Slifka Foundation and its president, Riva Ariella Ritvo-Slifka; the Amazon Literary Partnership; the Ballard Spahr Foundation; *Copper Nickel*; the McKnight Foundation; the National Endowment for the Arts; the National Poetry Series; the Target Foundation; and other generous contributions from foundations, corporations, and individuals. Also, this activity is made possible by the voters of Minnesota through a Minnesota State Arts Board Operating Support grant, thanks to a legislative appropriation from the arts and cultural heritage fund. For a full listing of Milkweed Editions supporters, please visit milkweed.org.

milkweed
editions

Founded as a nonprofit organization in 1980, Milkweed Editions is an independent publisher. Our mission is to identify, nurture and publish transformative literature, and build an engaged community around it.

Milkweed Editions is based in Bde Ota Othúŋwe (Minneapolis) within Mni Sota Makhoče, the traditional homeland of the Dakota people. Residing here since time immemorial, Dakota people still call Mni Sota Makhoče home, with four federally recognized Dakota nations and many more Dakota people residing in what is now the state of Minnesota. Due to continued legacies of colonization, genocide, and forced removal, generations of Dakota people remain disenfranchised from their traditional homeland. Presently, Mni Sota Makhoče has become a refuge and home for many Indigenous nations and peoples, including seven federally recognized Ojibwe nations. We humbly encourage readers to reflect upon the historical legacies held in the lands they occupy.

milkweed.org

Interior design by Tijqua Daiker
Typeset in Bulmer

Bulmer was created in the late 1780s or early 1790s.
This late "transitional" typeface was designed
by William Martin for William Bulmer,
who ran the Shakespeare Press.